The Minister's Wife

Sharon Wright-Palmer

Revelation
Publishing

2012

The Minister's Wife

Sharon Wright-Palmer

First Edition: October 2012

ISBN 978-1-908293-18-3

Published by:

Revelation Publishing
B 1502
PO Box 15113
Birmingham
B2 2NJ
United Kingdom

www.revelationpublishing.com

ask@revelationpublishing.com

Contents

About the Author

Sharon is an anointed woman of God. She was born in London, England, and was saved at the age of sixteen. She had the opportunity to operate in various capacities within the church, such as Sunday school teacher, President/ member of the Youth Board and assisting in imparting the word God.

She is a nurse by profession and has completed a Master's Degree in Business Administration.

Sharon has been married to an Ordained Minister, Everet Palmer, for 18 years. They have three children, Ruth, Everet jr and Joseph.

One of her aspirations is to reach and teach women of all races, creeds, cultures and ethnicities that Jesus loves them just the way they are. It doesn't matter how daunting the past has been, there is great hope. "You were made in the likeness of God" (Genesis 1:27). "And He who has begun a good work in you, is faithful and just to complete it until the day of Jesus Christ" (Philippians 1:6).

She has many wishes but none greater than being an accomplished woman of God, enabling men and women to fulfil their destiny in the Kingdom of God.

Dedication

This book is dedicated to all people of God around the world, who are seeking the "will" of God for their lives, and need a source of inspiration to go forward.

This book is a tool for Ministers' wives who have served in the ministry, and for those who are currently serving or planning to serve. It is also aimed at congregational members. By reading this book, you will gain an insight into the life of a Minister's wife along with some of the issues she has to undergo from time to time. It will furthermore demonstrate what she has to do to encourage herself, her family, church members and friends.

Also, an awareness will be developed as to how to treat her, how you can help her remain strong in ministry, and how to encourage and support her to maximise her true potential in Christ Jesus

Acknowledgements

With special thanks:

To God for giving me the strength and the ability to write this book.

To my husband Everet for his unfading love.

To my daughter Ruth for her poems and encouragement.

To my sons Everet jr and Joseph for their love and understanding whilst I was writing this book.

To my cousin Jennifer Miller and Camlakay for assisting in reading some of the scripts.

To Evadney Ellis for taking the time to read the entire scripts.

To my sister Paulette, Rev and Mrs R. Robinson for their prayers and encouragement.

To Mrs Daphne Scott and Rev Beryl R. Thompson whose life I have admired over the many years.

To all the women of God who have shared their life stories and the desires of their heart.

The Minister's Wife

You are reading this book for a good reason! It is not a mere coincidence that you have extended your hands and touched it. As your shimmering eyes plunge into these wonderful words they will help to mould your spiritual life. I have been having a burning passion for the people of God, especially ministers' wives. I have been crying out to the Lord for help and support on their behalf. Throughout the years the wisdom I have obtained is now being written in book form to mentor other ministers' wives. Too many ministers' wives have been serving the church and need someone to lend a hand every now and then.

You are not reading this book by chance. Your life is concealed with Christ in God, therefore; you are a very special person who was bought with a price, the precious blood of Jesus Christ. You are an heir of God and a joint heir with Christ, and you are more than a conqueror. A successful person with passion and drive, destined to win, and you must go forth in fulfilling your purpose and destiny in God, which will bring forth fruit, fulfilment and overwhelming joy.

As you read this book, it will open your eyes to some of the issues ministers' wives have experienced. I hope this book will reassure and inspire. It is based on some true life-stories that have been shared by conversing with a number of Ministers' wives. However, I have changed the scenarios in order to maintain anonymity so that individuals cannot be identified. I do hope it will help you to see these ladies from a different perspective and that you will endeavour to value them, and to treat them with respect and dignity.

The Values of a Minister's wife

For this reason a man shall leave his father and mother and be joined to his wife and the two shall be one flesh" (Matthew 19:5). That means, "What God has joined together, let no man separate" (Matthew 19:6). She is therefore, "Bone of my bone and flesh of my flesh she shall be called woman" (Genesis 2:23). She becomes the "crown for her husband" (Proverbs 12:4).

Who sees her? Who recognises her values? Who knows her intent? Who upholds her in prayers? The minister and his wife have been married for some time, they love, cherish and adore each other, yet in all this astounding time they are faced with challenges and the pressures of life and the question that occasionally comes to mind; Has the right decision been made in marrying a Minister of the Gospel? "One of the strongest elements in spiritual warfare and in the exercise of authority is married couples in harmony and unity".[1]

The work of a minister's wife has never been an easy task. Yet critics would make rash decisions in judging her. What is he doing with her? She does not dress right, she is ugly, she is uneducated, she is not minister material, she does not support her husband's ministry, she is unsociable; and the list goes on.

---

1   Derek Prince, Husbands and Fathers: Rediscover the creator's purpose for men, (Chosen Books, Great Britain, 2000), p.49

The wife of the minister shoulders the grunts of her husband, she is the one who sees him out of his "suit" the unfinished product, and of course you see him the finished product, when he comes in his suit and tie, for example. Where were they when he was under that Juniper tree? This Juniper tree here represents fears, discouragements, isolations and anxieties. Elijah was running away from Jezebel He said, "It is enough Lord I want to die" (1 Kings 19:4). Where were they when Delilah brought distraction? This symbolizes falsehood, loneliness, deception and apprehension. Joseph was soon in trouble through no fault of his own. Mrs Potiphar wants to seduce him while Potiphar is at work. Joseph said, "How can I do this great wickedness and sin against God?" (Genesis 39:9). It surely takes a woman of passion, love, courage and concern to look out for her husband and to make clear to him that trouble that is ahead. She is his mentor, his evaluator, his censor, and helper. I believe that it is the desire of every women of God to see her husband excel in his ministry. She is his wife who is created in the "image of God" (Genesis 1:27).

In Proverbs the Bible rightly sums her up,

"She is more precious than rubies, and all the things you may desire cannot compare with her. Length of days is in her right hand, in her left hand riches and honour. Her ways are ways of pleasantness and all her paths are peace. She is a tree of life to those who take hold of her, and happy are all who retain her" (Proverbs 3:14-18).""

"Who can find a virtuous and capable wife? She is worth more than precious rubies. Her husband can trust her, and she will greatly enrich his life. She will not hinder him but help him all his life. She finds wool and flax and busily spins it. She is like a merchant's ship; she brings her food from afar. She gets up before dawn to prepare breakfast for her household and plan the day's work for her servant girls. She goes out to inspect a field and buys it; with her earnings she plants a vineyard. She is energetic and strong, a hard worker, she watches for bargains; her lights burn late into night. Her hands are busy spinning thread, her fingers twisting fibre. She extends a helping hand to the poor and opens her arms to the needy. She has no fear of winter for her household because all of them have warm clothes. She quilts her own bedspreads.

She dresses like royalty in gown of finest cloth. Her husband is well known, for he sits in the council meeting with the other civic leaders. She makes belted linen garments sashes to sell to the merchants. She is clothed with strength and dignity and she laughs with no fear of the future when she speaks. Her words are wise and kindness is the rule when she gives instruction, she carefully watches all that goes on in her household and does not have to bear consequences of laziness. Her children stand and bless her, her husband praises her, there are many virtuous and capable women in the world, but you surpass them all. Charm is deceptive and beauty does not last but a woman who fears the Lord will be greatly praised. Reward her for all she has done, let her deeds publicly declare her praise" (Proverbs 31:10-31).

How marvellous, uplifting, absorbing, sobering and encouraging these magnificent words are coming from the book of Proverbs. It is a correct summary, and a reflection of true women of God.

Without a doubt, "A man's greatest treasure is in is wife she is a gift from the Lord" (Proverbs 18:22).

Undeniably, the way of life for a minister's wife can be very challenging every now and then, but there is always great hope for the people of God; a hope which makes us not ashamed. In (1John 3:2-3) it says, "Beloved now we are the children of God! And it has not yet been revealed what we shall be, but we know that when He revealed, we shall be like Him, for we shall see Him as He is and everyone who has this hope in Him purifies himself, just as He is pure". Joel adds, "The Lord will never bring His children to shame" (Joel 2:26).

For this reason, I truly believe in order for the minister's wife to survive in the ministry she needs the anointing of the Holy Spirit. Without the leading of the Holy Spirit she will find it even more difficult to cope with some of the uncertainties and tests that are ahead. In (Zechariah 4:6) we are reminded, "It is not by might or by power but it is by God's Spirit".

The Importance of the Holy Spirit in the Life of the Minister's wife

The Holy Spirit is for everyone who believes in the Lord Jesus Christ. "The Holy Spirit comes to live in us when we receive Jesus and are born again of the Spirit. The baptism in the Holy Spirit is the pouring out of the Spirit. We cannot expect Him to pour out through us until He is living in us. So before we ask to be baptized of the Holy Spirit, we must first be sure that we have indeed received the Lord Jesus as saviour and invite Him to live in us by His Spirit".[2]

The Holy Spirit, in reality, is a person with feelings and emotions. Henceforth, it is imperative that we recognize Him as the most influential creator of our lives. The Holy Spirit gives life (John 6:63), He lives within us (Romans. 8:11), He guides us (John 16:13), He teaches us (John 14:26), and He empowers us (Acts 1:8). In actual fact, whatever we are lacking in this life, the Holy Spirit can empower us to do exceptionally well. "Most of the time the Holy Spirit's power is released in your life in quiet, unassuming ways that you aren't even aware of or can't feel. He often nudges us with a gentle whisper". We must, "cooperate with the Holy Spirit's work because the Holy Spirit releases His power the moment you take a step of faith". [3]

2   Dennis and Rita Bennett, The Holy Spirit and You, 1st, Ed, (Kingsway Publication, Great Britain,1985), p.40

3   Rick Warren, The Purpose Driven Life: What on Earth am I Here For? (Zondervan, United State of America, 2002), p.174

Unquestionably, the Holy Spirit is very much alive, He can undo everything that seems impossible and makes the impossible possible. How inspirational! Awesome are the mighty works of the Holy Spirit in the lives of the believers. "The chief role of the Holy Spirit in the process of our salvation is to make us one with Christ".[4] When Jesus was about to leave His disciples He promised unto them another comforter - the Holy Spirit.

One of the most eloquent biblical passages that describe the Holy Spirit is found in (Acts 2:1-4),

"When the day of Pentecost was fully come; they were all in one accord in one place; and suddenly there came a sound from heaven as of a rushing mighty wind and it filled the whole house where they were sitting; then there appeared to them divided tongues as of fire and one sat upon each of them; and they were filled with the Holy Spirit".

The Holy Spirit's greatest product is the word of God coming from the Bible. If we want to be on good terms with the Bible we must agree with the Holy Spirit. Whilst in concurrence with the Holy Spirit we need to stay in our anointing and not withdraw from it. Having the Holy Spirit within our lives we are able to do extraordinary

4 Anthony A. Hoekema, Saved by Grace, 1st Ed, (Wm. B. Eerdmans publishing co, 1989), p.28

things in our everyday proceedings. So why are we acting as though we are defeated?

As though we are mediocre? On the contrary we are the head and not the tail (Ephesians 1:22), the victor and not the victim (Psalm 20:8), the righteousness of God (Romans 1:17), a royal priesthood (1Peter 2:9), the salt of the earth (Matthew 5:13), and the light of the world (Matthew 5:14). Rightfully, we ought to be involved in making decisions that will affect our world today in a positive way. "The men of Issachar had understanding of the times to know what Israel ought to do" (1 Chronicles 12:32). They were the decision makers. They were the strategists of their time. "A word fitly spoken in due season is like an apple of gold in settings of silver" (Proverbs 25:11). Remember, "It is a sin to know what you ought to do and then not do it". (James 4:17).

Some ways in which the Holy Spirit can be released into our lives are through our words, praying in tongues and being obedient unto God.

By Our Words

The words that come from our mouth are very effective. In the Gospel of (Mark 7:15) we read, "There is nothing that enters a man from outside which can defile him, but the things which come out of him, those are the things that defile him". In saying that, we have to be very careful of the words that we speak. Don't be negative. If we are negative with our words it gets us nowhere. Why then are we so negative?

There are so many bad reports in and around us from secular news reports let us not add to them. The Bible says in (Numbers 13:18-20;30-31), Moses according to God's instruction, sent men to spy out the land of Canaan, "to see what the land is like, whether the people who dwell in it are strong or weak, few or many; good or bad, and rich or poor".

In spite of the giants, Joshua and Caleb brought back good reports. "We are well able to possess the land". The others were very negative they delivered bad reports to Moses. Did they possess the land? The naysayers did not! Their fear, unbelief, and negative report cost them a Divine inheritance. (Numbers 14:31) clearly states that by doubting the Almighty they "refused" their blessing. Nonetheless, it was only Joshua and Caleb, and believers found worthy by God, who were able to reach and enter the promised land.

(Proverbs 18:21) tells us, "Death and life are in the power of the tongue". Ours words can either build us up or tear us down. As we speak the words of God daily, the Holy Spirit takes those words and brings them to pass. In (Acts 10:44) we read, "While He spoke these words, the Holy Spirit fell upon all those who were listening".

In (Matthew 16:19) Jesus said, "I will give you the keys of the kingdom of heaven and whatever you bind on earth will be bound in heaven and whatever you loose on earth will be loosed in heaven" (1 John 5:15). "We know that He hears us and whatever we ask, we know we have the petitions that we have asked of Him". Lord, "Let the words of my mouth and the mediation of my heart be acceptable in your sight, Oh Lord my strength and my Redeemer" (Psalm 19:14).

Women of God, we can change the quality and the direction of our lives by the words we speak. Let us remain positive, it will renew daily our faith and build strong characters within us.

Pray in Tongues

Praying in tongues is an act of great magnitude. From the scripture (1 Corinthians 14:2) it notifies us, "He who speaks in a

tongue does not speak to men but to God for no one understands Him, however, in the spirit he speaks mysteries". "Praying in tongues edifies [us]" (1 Corinthians 14:4). The Holy Spirit releases powers within us, so we are made stronger in God, and in our weakness He enables us to do extraordinary things. Praying in tongues confuses the enemy and helps to destroy his plans; he doesn't understand the language used. So as believers; we must endeavour to use our heavenly language and let the Holy Spirit plead our case on our behalf before the Father. In (Ephesians 6:18) we read, "Never stop praying especially for others. Always pray by the power of the Spirit".

According to (Romans 8:26-27), "For we do not know what we should pray for as we ought, but the Spirit Himself makes intercession for us with groaning which cannot be uttered. And He that searched the hearts knows what the mind of the Spirit is, because He makes intercession for the saints according to the will of God".

As we pray in tongues, The Holy Spirit takes this language and interprets it for us. Praying in tongues gives us extra strength and in principle demonstrates God's perfect will through our lives. The will of God in heaven infiltrates and invades the earth as we pray in our heavenly language.

Being Obedient to God

Paul admonished us In (Acts 5:32) saying, God gives the Holy Spirit to those who obey Him. Of a truth, we know that the Holy Spirit is a gift from God. If we constantly obey God He will release the power of the Holy Spirit in our lives. We are again reminded in the Gospel of Luke,

"The Spirit of the Lord is upon me because He has anointed me to preach the gospel to the poor; He has sent me to heal the brokenhearted. To proclaim liberty to the captives and recovery of sight to the blind, to set at liberty those who are oppressed; to proclaim the acceptable year of the Lord" (Luke 4:18-19).

How satisfying are the mighty works of God! His words are so powerful. What Joy it is to be able to experience the manifestation of the Holy Spirit in our own personal life. Individuals who are heartbroken are made whole, those who are oppressed are being set free, and those who are sick are made well in Jesus Christ.

The results of the Holy Spirit in our lives; He brings us joy and laughter, He gives supernatural guidance, and He brings us blessing in our Household.

He Brings Joy and Laughter

As children of God it is one of our desires to maintain joy and laughter in our lives. Not everyone can say that they have joy and laughter in their everyday walk. Sometimes there are pains, tears and sorrows. In (Psalm 42:11) David said, "Why are you cast down, O my soul? Hope in God". As believers in the faith, we know that by obeying God's words we will be able to experience His everlasting joy and His strength in our lives. How inspiring!

According to (Psalm 16:11) it says, "In the presence of the Lord is fullness of joy; at your right hand there is pleasure for evermore".

"Honour and majesty you have placed upon Him; for you have made Him most blessed forever" (Psalm 21:5-6). "When the Lord brought back the captives to Zion, we were like men who dreamed, our mouths were filled with laughter, our tongues with songs of joy" (Psalm 126:1-2).

Laughter is wonderful, if we could only give God the permission to put His passion inside us, we would behold His never-ending joy and gladness. Let it be, to us, dear Lord according to your words. Continue to dwell in God's presence and enjoy His glory.

He Gives Supernatural Guidance

The Lord always gives supernatural guidance. When the children of Israel were leaving Egypt to go the promised land, on their journey the Egyptians pursued them, with all the horses and chariots of Pharaoh. When Pharaoh drew near, the children became so afraid. So Moses said to them in (Exodus 14:13-14),

"Do not be afraid, stand still and see the salvation of the Lord which He will accomplish for you today. For the Egyptians whom you see today, you shall see again no more forever. The Lord shall fight for you and you shall hold your peace".

The children of Israel had victory; they were guided and guarded by the mighty hands of

God. They were able to cross over safely on dry land. How great is our God! He has done it and He will do it again. It was David who said "I have been young and now am old but I have not seen the righteous forsaken, or His seed begging for bread" (Psalm37:25). Keep holding on, victory is just ahead, we are nearer than when we first began. God is a triumphant God. He has never lost a battle and He has no intention of losing one now. He is the "Alpha and Omega, the Beginning and the End" (Revelation 21:6). And He reigns for evermore.

Once more, we read in 2 Chronicles that the enemies came against Jehoshaphat to battle. He became so terrified because he knew that his army was not strong enough to defeat the enemies. He did not know what to do, so he gathered all the people together and started praying.

"O Lord, God of our fathers, are you not God in heaven? And do you not rule over all the kingdoms of the nations? In your hand are power and might, so that none is able to withstand you" (2 Chronicles 20:6)

The Spirit of the Lord came up on Jahaziel a Levite in the midst of the assembly.

"He said, Hearken, all Judah, you inhabitants of Jerusalem, and King Jehoshaphat. The Lord says this to you: Be not afraid or dismayed at this great multitude; for the battle is not yours, but God's" (2 Chronicles 20:15).

Believer, in the light of 2 Chronicles we are told that Jehoshaphat believed the prophetic word, and went out to battle. They did not have to fight, instead they worshiped the Lord, "Singing songs and giving praises to Him" (2 Chronicles 20:22). The victory was theirs. Does God still speak to His people today? Yes. In the mists of dilemmas, God will send a prophetic word through His servant. Hang on in there, your financial situation may be looking bleak, you may be having difficulty with your children, your health may be failing, and your marriage may be on the rocks etc. Remember, God will never "lie" (Numbers 23:19). He can restore your marriage, re-establish your finances, bring healing to your health; and the children. God never fails, continue to trust in Him, you need not fight, just give Him praise and worship and you will see the deliverance of the Lord.

He Brings Blessing in Our Household

Blessings on our families are what every believer craves and hopes for. These can only come to us through our Lord, and saviour, Jesus Christ. He is the Bread of Life (John 6:48), the Lily of the Valleys (Songs of Songs. 2:1), and the Bright and Morning Star (Revelation 22:16).

In (2 Samuel 6:11) we read, "The Ark of the Lord remained in the House of Obed-Edom the Gittite for three months and the Lord blessed Obed-Edom and all his household".

Believers, when we dwell in the presence of the Lord there is always a certainty, that we will receive abundant blessings, "The blessing of the Lord makes rich and adds no sorrow with it" (Proverbs.10:22). What more can we ask for? This blessing is not always about money, it is also about good health, and peace of mind, allowing even our very enemies to be at peace with us. "Blessed is everyone that feared the Lord; that walked in His ways, for thou shall eat the labour of thine hands; happy shall thou be, and it shall be well with thee" (Psalm 128:1-2).

In the book of (Acts 1:8) Jesus says,

"But you shall receive power, when the Holy Spirit has come upon you and you shall be my witnesses in Jerusalem and all Judea and Samaria and to the ends of the earth".

How awesome is the book of Acts of the Apostles, to the believers. We have been given super-natural power. Which means our difficult situations can be rejuvenated. We have been set free from fear, guilt, doubt, anxiety and stress. In all honesty, the Holy Spirit is not just for one day but for every day of the week, month and year. What a privilege? What an opportunity?

Ordinary people like you and I can do extraordinary things. How awe-inspiring is this?

Here is a list of Bible women of faith who had some difficult times in life. These women have overcome great trial and tribulation, yet, their lives have been a success, and today we can testify that they have made a difference to our lives, our children, our family and to our world.

Ruth

Ruth was a great grandmother of David. She was a girl from the country of Moab. She was married, but soon after her husband died. She stepped out by faith and left her own people to go with her mother-in-law to Bethlehem. In Bethlehem, she was a stranger, the only thing she had was her mother-in- law. Because of her sincerity, commitment and determination Ruth experienced acts of kindness.

Ruth said to her mother-in-law, "Entreat me not to leave you or to turn back from following you, for where you go I will go, where you lodge I will lodge. Your people shall be my people and Your God my God" (Ruth 1:16).

Women of God, sometimes in order for us to reach our destiny we need to take that step of faith in order to gain God's favour.

Esther

Esther was a Jewish girl who was living with her cousin Mordecai. When Queen Vashti was banished in disgrace Esther became Queen. Haman who was then King Xerxes' new prime minister requested that all people should bow before him but Mordecai refused. Haman was furious with the Jewish rebel; he was determined to punish not only Mordecai but the Jewish race. It was Queen Esther who risked her life when she went before the king.

Esther sent a message to Mordecai, "Gather all the Jews that are present in Shushan and fast for me, neither eat nor drink for three days, night or day. I also and my maids will fast as you do. Then I will go to the King though it is against the law; "If I perish I perish" (Esther. 4:15-16).

Esther, a woman of destiny, understood something that was crucial to herself and her people. She knew it was time to go forward, and to believe God for the future. "Some trust in chariots, and horses, but we will remember the name of the Lord our God. They have bowed down and fallen; but we have risen and stand upright" (Psalm 20:7-8). Esther was victorious through Jesus Christ.

Sarah

Sarah, the mother of nations supported her husband on a journey to fulfil God's plans. Even though Sarah and Abraham were extremely rich in livestock, silver and gold they were missing one thing. It was a "child". It was not an easy task for Sarah to leave her relatives but she obeyed, honoured, and loved her husband; she even called him "Lord" (1 Peter 3:6). Years went by and she still didn't have a child, she even laughed at the idea of having a son at an old age. Although God's promises sounded impossible, God's plans were accomplished.

"Sarah became pregnant and bore Abraham a son in his old age at the set time God told him.

Abraham named his son whom Sarah bore to him Isaac" (Genesis 21:2-3).

Women of faith, Sarah had nothing to lose but so much to gain. She put her trust in God and it paid off.

Deborah

After Ehud died, the Israelites once again did evil in the eyes of the Lord. So the Lord sold them into the hands of Jabin a king of Canaan, who reigned in Hazor. The commander of this army was Sisera. Deborah a prophetess was leading Israel at that time. She sent for Barak and said to him,

"The Lord the God of Israel commands you to go, take with you ten thousand men. Barak said to her, if you go with me I will go; but if you don't go with me I won't go. Very well Deborah said. I will go with you but because of the way you are going about this, the honour will not be yours. For the Lord will hand Sisera over to a woman" (Judges 4:8-9).

Deborah knew what Israel ought to do to defeat Sisera; she was a woman of vision. She gave instruction to Barak which lead the Israelites to victory. God is looking for women who He can trust to carry out His plans. We too can make ourselves available for Him to pilot us in the right way.

There are other women in the Bible that I could have mentioned. They too were of tremendous blessing. Nonetheless, I have chosen these four women of faith and hope. Looking at the life of these women I have noticed that they had their own identity and remain unique in their own rights. On the other hand, they have some common factors among them:

- They loved God and they loved people

- They were sincere and committed

- They had a passion to serve

- They were fearless, willing and determined

- They were positive about themselves

- They were victorious in whatever they were doing

- They made themselves available to be used by God

- They were just ordinary women, which God used to do extraordinary things.

Like Deborah, Esther, Ruth, and Sarah, we too can make a difference in our own personal lives, in our family, in our community and in our world. Today, natural people are becoming supernatural beings because of Jesus Christ, who lives and reigns. These women have demonstrated commitment and strong determination.

Did they make a difference? Oh yes they did. Were they victorious? Oh yes they were. Can we make a difference? Yes it is feasible, "We can do all things through Christ who enables us" (Philippians 4:13). It only takes a willing, a devoted and an unwavering person to make the first step and then God will demonstrate His super natural power in and through us.

The Minister's Wife and Her Apparel

I lost my dear mother a few months ago; this caused much pain, sorrow and heartache. It was a very stressful time for my family and I. Despite my grief, during that time; we visited a certain fellowship. I was not wearing a hat on my head. As I sat in the congregation an elderly lady approached me and the first word from her mouth was, "You don't dress like a minister's wife". Can you imagine how I felt at that moment in time? It was not a nice feeling. Losing my dear mother, all I needed was someone to say a kind word. Thank God for His mercy, I was able to correct her but how many people are as bold as I am to challenge critics.

A few months later I revisited the same congregation, and this time I was wearing a hat. Yes, she was there and this time, she complimented me, saying, "You certainly look like a minister's wife today, lovely hat". Regrettably, for some legalists, it is how big your hat or how long your dress that makes you Christ like. God is looking for true worshippers. In John's Gospel He indicated, "God is a Spirit and those who worship Him, must worship Him in Spirit and in Truth" (John 4:24).

God is not looking for people who can impress Him with their style of dressing. I guess covering one's head is of paramount importance for some believers, this might be their conviction. I am not knocking that, but for some believers it's never an issue. In (1 Peter 3:3-4) its tells us, "Do not let your adornment be merely outward, arranging the hair, wearing gold, or putting on fine apparel, rather let it be the hidden person of the heart, with the incorruptible beauty of a gentle and quiet spirit". "The Lord does not make decisions the way we do; people judge by our outward appearance, but the Lord looks at a person's thoughts and intentions" (1 Samuel 16:7).

We need to let the beauty of Jesus be seen in us. For example, loving God and loving people. It doesn't matter what age we are, where we come from, what we look like, God still values us, and He wants to renew our strength so that we can fulfil our purpose and destiny in life. "Never forget that life is not about you, you exist for God's purposes. Not vice versa".[5] Yes, you are not your own, you belong to God.

"The vast majority of believers spend their entire lives fixing up, painting up, and adorning the exterior of the house only, many are content to stay in the outer court. It is not God's desire that we remain in the outer court; He wants us to come all the way in so that we can enjoy full fellowship with Him".[6]

In (John 4:23) Jesus said,

---

5   Rick Warren, The Purpose Driven Life: What on Earth am I Here For? (Zondervan, USA, 2002), p.173

6   James W Goll, The Lost Art of Practicing His Presence, (Destiny Image Publishers, USA, 2005), p.62

"The time is coming and is already here, when by the power of God's Spirit people will worship the Father as He really is, offering Him the true worship that He wants". Let us be submissive, and commit ourselves to the Most High God, by making it our priority to worship Him in Spirit and in Truth. He is worthy and wonderful and it's the true worship that we give that really affirms who we are in Him. As faith believers, we must make an effort to do what is required to bear good fruit. Read and study the word of God, and allow the scripture to guide, and guard us in the right pathway, focused on God.

In (Galatians 5:22-23) Paul indicated,

"The fruit of the Spirit is love, joy, peace, longsuffering, gentleness, goodness, faith, meekness, and self-control". In view of that, the fruits of the Spirit have enough spiritual ingredients in them to enhance our lives, how we align our lives with the word of God, will greatly impact on our destiny. "If you've not been bearing the fruit of the Spirit in your life the way you'd like, ask God to help you plant good seeds and pull up any weeds that may have grown up around your soul".[7] It is God's desire to draw us into a place of intimacy where His grace will allow us to submit to the work of His Spirit in our lives.

---

7   Stormie Omartian, Just Enough Light for the step I'm on, 1st Ed, (Harvest House Publishers, 2002) p.121

True Life Experiences of Minister's Wives

As mentioned earlier, I have changed the scenarios in order to maintain anonymity so that individuals cannot be identified.

1: Jane and Joespeh

Jane and Joseph met when they were in their final year at University. Soon after graduation they got married, and had two beautiful children. Approximately five years after, Joseph felt the call of God on his life, so his wife agreed, and shortly after he went off to Bible School. She remained in her job and assisted him whilst he was at Bible School. After three years he graduated and began pastoring a church. Her husband is now doing well in the ministry, but, she says, "In her early years of their ministry an individual looked at her and said in a soft-spoken voice, "Your husband is looking so young and handsome, you seem to be older than him".

The words spoken has had negative impact on her life, on several occasions, it has caused her to feel emotionally very low about herself. In the midst of this, she didn't feel she could trust anyone to share the problem with. After all she feels she should be the one to encourage others. Had she not been a prayerful person, she would certainly have become caught up with other people's perception of her. On the other hand, she had to get on with her responsibilities within the church. As the minister's wife, her feelings, fears and tears were never known.

Woman of faith, do not be dismayed, do not give up, and do not give in. You were uniquely designed by God to carry out His purpose. You have stood beside your dear husband through thick and thin, you have looked after the children whilst he got on with his studies. You are favourable in the sight of God. Be strong and be of a good courage. Do not allow your critics to distract you. Look at the story of Nehemiah, who was a man of prayer. When he heard about the broken walls of Jerusalem, he wept. Still, he decided to rebuild the walls. When Sanballat and Tobiah heard of it, they laughed and mocked him, many unkind words were said. In spite of the fierce opposition Nehemiah stood his ground and re-built the walls of Jerusalem. He said, "I am doing a great work, how can I come down?" (Nehemiah 6:3).

You are doing a great work; do not let anyone or anything bring you distraction. You are on a mission for the Most High God, do not be distracted and discouraged by unkind words, you can never be disadvantaged, God is your advantage.

In (Romans 8:31) Paul encourages,

"What shall we then say to these things? If God be for us, who can be against us?" (Isaiah

54:17) confirms, "No weapon formed against you shall prosper and every tongue which rises against you in judgement you shall condemn. This is the heritage of the servants of the Lord".

Weapons may develop, and discharge but they will never overthrow you, because the Holy Spirit will deny access. You are hidden with Christ in God (Colossians 3:3), and you are a winner. In (Isaiah 43:13) God said, "He will not allow Satan to pluck you out of His hand, before the day was He was, He works and no one will reverse it". I encourage you to "be strong, vigorous and very courageous, be not afraid, neither be dismayed, for the Lord your God is with you wherever you go" (Joshua 1:9).

Did you know the blessing of the Lord brings attention? It makes you look and feel good and causes you to excel. I encourage you therefore, to enjoy God's blessings and don't be concerned about fault-finders.

2: Valarie and Tom

Valarie told me she had been married for forty-five years to Tom. They had five lovely children. Tom's pastoral position takes him overseas, at least two to three times per year. She said, "When the children were younger, this was a great problem to them. His sons especially used to cry tirelessly whenever he went away". As for her there were lots of lonely nights, and she used to wish there was another way. She was reminded on several occasions by others, "She was not from a Christian family and that she was lucky to have married a minister of religion". The humiliation that she "endured" from nit-pickers was revolting at times. There were times when she was suffering from low self-esteem and even found herself agreeing with them through negative self-talk. She said, "Where I come from, my father, mother, brothers and sisters are not believers in the faith". She got saved at the age of 15 years and was the only Christian in her immediate family. Had she not believed in praying, fasting, reading the Bible and believing the word of God, her life would not have been what it is now. She is a product of God's blessings.

Woman of destiny, be encouraged, you are an anointed woman of God, it does not matter from what background you are coming from, let not the limitation of the past and how you were raised determine your future. Do not despise small beginnings, for God uses those who are available, not only those who are capable. It is God who has been your refuge and strength, and He will surely give you additional strength to go forward. Do not be disappointed; do not be weary in well doing, His eyes are always watching over you, He cares enough that He sent His only son Jesus Christ to set you free.

In (Jeremiah 1:5) Jesus said, "Before I formed you in the womb I knew you; before you were born I sanctified you". In (Hebrews 13:5) Jesus declares, "I will never leave you or forsake you". In (Psalm 139:14) David says, "I will praise the Lord because I am fearfully and wonderfully made, marvellous are your works Lord".

You are who you are in Christ Jesus. Do not let fault-finders tell you otherwise, you are precious in God's sight and if God says so, that's who you are.

Do verbalize some positive words over your life daily. Such as, God is my refuge and my fortress (Psalm 91:2). The Lord of Hosts is with me (Psalm 46:11). I am the righteousness of God (Psalm 64:10). God is my defence (Psalm 62:6). In Him I dwell (Psalm 91:1). And have peace (Philippians 4:7). He is my shepherd I shall not want (Psalm 23:1). He shall supply all my need according to His riches in glory by Christ Jesus (Philippians 4:19) and I will love Him, because He had head my voice and my supplications (Psalm 116:1). Praise the Lord (Psalm 117:1-2). His truth endures forever.

"No matter how difficult your life might be, there is great news for you. You are not a helpless victim caught between two nearly equal but opposite heavenly super-powers".[8] God can

---
8   Neil T Anderson, Steps to Freedom in Christ, 1st Ed, (United Kingdom, 2003) p.9

use whom He chooses to carry out His plans and purposes and no one can stop this. He is altogether God and none of us is hopeless in His sight, we are His children.

One of the greatest protections against nit-pickers is to have a fervent love relationship with God through which you grow to know Him personally. God's power will then be made known as you grow to be His true reflection.

3: Amy and Peter

Amy was married to Peter for thirty-two years. When they got married he told her often, of how much he loved her, and that she was God's gift to him. Two years ago, he left her for another woman. He complained and said, "She was not as beautiful as before because she had increased in size, and I want to be with someone much younger".

She said, "When this happened it caused a lot of ill feeling within the family and close friends." It also caused enormous shame in their congregation and other fellowships that they had ministered to in the past. They were also affected as it brought disillusionment and shock. Their children were so upset that they refused to attend church. At times she could not pray, and even if she attempted to pray she just could

---

not utter a word from her mouth. For days she was too distressed to pick herself up. She experienced chronic headaches; her tears flowed like an immeasurable torrent. There was so much grief; words were just inadequate to explain. Loneliness haunted her day and night. She just could not talk to anyone, and she did not want any one from outside of her immediate family to question her about the affair. She was too ashamed to talk about it. She carried this pain for days all by herself. With her family she finally found a way of coping with the unhappiness. They fasted and prayed and the Lord gave them strength and courage. Today, she is still in the faith with a ministry which involves praise and worship and her children still love the Lord.

Woman of God, according to (Ecclesiastes 9:11) "The race is neither for the swift nor the battle for the strong". Do not be disheartened, be of good cheer. Some believers do walk out of the "will" of God there are no two ways about that. Some have the opportunity to mend their ways, others do not. The reality is, we have an opportunity to make choices be they good or bad, that's the way life is. Free will is what God gives us, and He will never force us to do otherwise. I am not here to judge this man of God, but it is your time to shine.

"An experienced Minister was once asked about a certain person. Is he a good Christian? The

Minister replied, I don't know; I can't tell you yet. I haven't met his wife. A husband's success is seen in his wife".[9] This might sound amusing and raise a few cheek bones with laughter here and there, but it carries a lot of weight. Let it not be said that you are still at home crying yourself to sleep at night. Having recurrent headaches and sleeping restlessly, because this is not good for anyone's health. Therefore, I urge you if you are not working get yourself a job, if not create one for yourself, be an employer. It is God who bestows creative ideas. If you are working, well done; now get yourself a nice hair do, if you haven't had one recently, not for one day but every day. Get yourself some manicures and pedicures; it's your time to glow. You are not rejoicing that he is gone but you need to get on with your life. Christ has already died for the human race. Hence, there's no need to die a second death. The price He paid was sufficient. This is not the end. It is a new beginning in your life; now start living as though you have a hope.

(Philippians 1:6) declares,

"Being confident of this very thing, that He who has begun a good work in you will complete it until the day of Jesus Christ".

---

9 Derek Prince, Husbands and Fathers: Rediscover the creator's purpose for men, (Chosen Books, Great Britain, 2000), p.33

A pastor that I know often says in his sermons, "One plus God is the majority". This means, if you have God on your side, you have already won the victory. Thus, you can say like Jeremiah, "God is my battle-axe and weapon of war" (Jeremiah 51:20).

Woman of Faith, stay blessed, the Bible says in (Romans 8:28), "And we know that all things work together for good to them that love the Lord, to them who are called according to his purpose".

This might sound a bit "harsh" but let us focus our attention to the story of Lazarus. He was dead for fourdays (John 11:14). Jesus could have gotten to Lazarus before he died but somehow He decided to delay for four days. Jesus had a plan. His plan was not to bring healing to Lazarus but to bring a resurrection. Jesus said, "I am the resurrection and the life, He who believes in me though he may die, he shall live. And whoever lives and believes in me shall never die" (John 11:25). Are you ready for a resurrection? Jesus is the answer; in Him you are healed and restored to your rightful position.

4: Mary and David

Mary said she had been married to David for forty years. They loved and cherished each other from the day they met. They had three children. They pastored many churches, around the globe. Her husband had a passion for souls and she was a great supporter and an encouragement to him. Eight years ago he was taken from her; he is now resting in the arms of our dear Lord and Saviour.

Mary said that from the moment he was taken from her she felt as though a part of her life had been lost. She said, "It has been eight years, but it seems as though it was yesterday". She is still feeling the grief, from time to time it lingers. She had great support from her children, but they could not fill his place. She said that the church had supported her in the first two to three months of her bereavement. This support gradually diminished. She thought they had forgotten her; the focus, she believes, was on David, not on the family. She assumes they were not as important as he was. She was "just" his wife and they were his children. She was so disappointed in the way she had been treated. She had spent so much of her time and effort supporting people around her, yet they had given little or no time to her. Had she not been a woman of prayer and faith, and someone who liked to read the word of God, she is not sure where she would be today. God be praised.

Woman of destiny, you may be going through situations that don't seem to make sense at times, but when you encounter such times, always remember that these are just stepping stones that will lead you to God's plans for your life.

The Bible says in (Psalm 27:10) "When your mother and father forsake you then the Lord will take you up". In the book of Isaiah we who are believers are also encouraged by Jesus.

"Fear not, for I have redeemed you; I have called you by your name; you are mine. When you pass through the waters I will be with you; and through the rivers; they shall not overflow you. When you walk through the fire you shall not be burned, nor shall the flame scorch you, for I am the Lord you God" (Isaiah 43:1-3).

What a consolation it is to know we are protected by the mighty hands of God. Let us take courage, God is not finished with you; it is not over until God says so. Let this psalm be a testimony:

"I waited patiently for the Lord, and He inclined to me, and heard my cry. He also brought me up out of a horrible pit, out of miry clay, and set my feet upon a rock, and established my steps. He put a new song in my mouth" (Psalm 40:1-2). "Praise the Lord of hosts for He is good, and His mercy endures forevermore" (Jeremiah 33:11).

Woman of Hope, continue to make Jesus the Lord and Saviour of your life. Refuse to accept failure in your life; you are a treasure God has entrusted "ministry" into your hands to bring deliverance, healing and salvation to your family, community and around the globe.

5: Anna and Peter

Anna and Peter had been married for forty four years. They had four beautiful girls and two handsome boys. Peter was the senior Pastor of the church. From the moment their children could walk and talk they were greatly involved in some church activities. Their first daughter got pregnant at the age of 25 years old. She had graduated from university with her profession. She wasn't married and was still living at home. Her mother said, "Approximately four to six weeks, in her pregnancy, Peter found out that his daughter was with child". He said, "The Holy Spirit had told him". Later the Church found out, and Peter had to step down from his pastoral position. She had to relinquish her church duties, and the children could no longer take part.

She said, "Peter became so miserable, it seems as though the peace of God had gone from their home". On account of that, their daughter had to leave the home to live with an aunt. Anna was traumatised, because she was torn between her daughter and her husband. As a wife she had to give support to Peter, as a mother, she had to be there for her daughter. She said she cried day and night to the Lord for help. She didn't know what to do. The only person that could comfort her in her time of needs was the Holy Spirit. She said, "He comes with a song over and over again, and from time to time a word just when I needed it". Her daughter gave birth after nine months. She had a lovely bouncing baby boy. She said, "In spite of the sorrows it was a happy ending". Her husband was restored to his rightful position as a senior Pastor, and the children and she were able to have fellowship again.

Woman of God, it is not an easy road we are travelling, but God is our help and guide in time of our troubles. He said, "Weeping may endure for a night but joy comes in the morning" (Psalm 30: 5).

(James 1:2-3) states that we should, "Count it all joy when we fall into various trials; knowing that the testing of our faith produces patience".

Keep on reinstating and re-establishing your relationship with God who is your daily provider in all things. Even though you have struggled with disappointment within your household, all is not lost. God is able, He assured us to, "Cast all our cares up on Him, because He cares for us" (1 Peter 5:7). On the other hand, "His yoke is easy and His burden is light" (Matthew11:30). Stay blessed. You can rest assured that the Lord will make a way for you even when you are in the wilderness.

The Faithful Wife

The minister's wife is a very vital person, to her husband and the ministry. She travels the lonely road, day after day, and in desperation, she learns to cry out to the Lord and follow Him through His word. She is his appraiser, his critic, his supporter and his encourager. She is able to give honest feedback on his sermons and other activities of ministry. "When a wife encourages her husband she is fulfilling the role of the Holy Spirit".[10] She is also the first person to tell him when he is not performing in a Godly manner and stays with him through the rough and the good times.

Many ministers, especially in the past, used to be called out on several occasions, early in the morning or late at nights to attend to the sick or any traumatic situations amongst members, and friends in the community. These hours were anti-social hours, but the minister's wife had to understand that it was her husband's duty regardless of how she felt. Although, this is all very demanding for her, the children and her husband, she has to learn to get on with her own life without complaining.

She will always encourage her husband to ensure that his friendship with members and others remains healthy and pure. So that

---

10 Derek Prince, Husbands and Fathers: Rediscover the creator's purpose for men, (Chosen Books, Great Britain, 2000), p.38

familiarity does not cause them to lose their respect for him as the man of God. She will also encourage him to avoid spending time alone with members of the opposite sex and to be aware of the language he uses in his day to day communications whether verbally, text messages, email and face book etc.

1 Thessalonians 5:21-22 admonishes us to,

"Hold fast to that which is good. Abstain from all appearance of evil". For she does not want to see his character tarnished, nor his ministry for the Gospel of the Lord and Saviour Jesus Christ brought into disrepute. Her husband at times may not appear to share her views but she says it in Love and ultimately it pays off. She is always praying for his ministry and she is aware that the Lord hears and answers prayers.

The minister's wife, has always enjoyed doing the work of the Lord, she suffers no resentment. She has confidence in God's words. The Lord has kept her. He has been her counsel and guide. She will continue to "praise the Lord with her whole heart and tell of all His marvellous works. She will be glad and rejoice in Him and sing praise to the Most High God" (Psalm 9:1-2).

Many churches have packed programmes thus causing the minister's wife to devote a lot of long hours at church, accompanied by the children. They often spend most of their week at church. On the weekdays, there may be activities on at least three evenings. These can be tiresome times for all. However, she feels that she has to support the programmes, or members will criticize her for not supporting her husband's ministry.

The children of ministers are oftentimes also, affected by his/her busy schedule. Some decide that they will never follow in their father's footsteps in ministry as the lack of quality time has caused a negative impact on their lives. Some feel that dad has time to attend funerals, counselling sessions, weddings, social meetings, business meetings, Bible studies, prayer meetings and other church activities but he does not make time for his family. As a result, the rearing of the children at times is left to the wife.

The work of a minister's wife never stops; she is generally there to support her husband through the good times and through the bad times.

Amidst the various telephone calls, disturbed sleep at nights, and lonesome days, she guards her heart against bitterness. Her eyes are upon the Lord in Him she takes refuge (Psalm 141:8). Her heart is overflowing with good things because she knows God reigns over all the earth. The Lord has searched her and knows her, He knows her sitting down and rising up;

and He understands her thought afar off (Psalm 139:1-2). The Lord has redeemed her soul (Psalm 34:22). And she will continue to bless the Lord with all her praise (Psalm 34:1). She devotes herself to support the people of God, her children, and her husband. She lovingly blesses her children with wise words, her prayers move heavy loads, her actions have made her marriage stronger, and her witness has won others for Christ.

She deepens herself with the word of God, because that is where she develops her personal relationship with Him and gathers daily strength. She sings songs of praise to cheer herself along the way. She believes in prayer and fasting and she uses it as a tool to get where she needs to go. She is loving and kind, always giving, and forever going the extra mile. She has many desires but none greater than having the quality of a godly woman.

The P.E.A.C.E. Factors

The minister's wife needs to be prayerful, encouraging, anointed, confidential, and she has to have endurance. Without these five factors she is going to undergo life in a more arduous way.

The Importance of Prayer

What is prayer? Prayer is a "Form of words, giving thanks or an appeal spoken to one's God".[11] Prayer is a spiritual "key" that opens the door of our hearts to God. This can be in words, with tears, a song or in tongues. Thus, our failure to reach the world for Christ is because we do not pray. "The prayer of a righteous man availed much" (James 5:16). It is through prayer that God moves and does miraculous works. "Elijah was a man with nature like ours, and he prayed earnestly that it would not rain; and it did not rain on the land for three years and six months. He prayed again, and the heaven gave rain and the earth produced its fruit" (James 5:17-18).

"Prayer is one of the means of releasing the ability of God".[12] Then, if God's ability is release in prayer, it stands to reason that there is no victory until we pray. For this reason we need to

---

11 Oxford English Dictionary, 1973

12 Charles Capps, Releasing The Ability Of God, (Harrison House publisher, Great Britain, 1978) p.125

take prayer seriously. When we pray, it allows us to have a successful and profitable life. Have you noticed, I didn't say a perfect life? This is because I don't believe that there is a perfect life on earth. For example, your husband or spouse may have a brilliant idea. The concept at first sounds great and looks good but somewhere in the conversation one party may use the word "but" be it the wife or the husband. This "but" causes doubt in the idea and sometimes may lead to disagreement. There is always personal opinion in marriage but it takes a prayerful woman of God to answer in a wise manner. She is not going to agree with her husband in everything he says or does, on the other hand, she is going to answer him in a respectful and wise manner that pleases him and turns back anger. This can only be achieved through continuous prayer.

(Proverbs 15:1) notes, "A soft answer turned away wrath; but grievous words stir up anger".

"We live in a world which is broken; a world which is not yet perfect, not in harmony with itself".[13] How else can we survive? It has to be through prayer, fasting, and our faith in God.

As a minister's wife I have been faced with lots of spiritual opposition. The devil is always on

---

13 Malcolm Goldsmith, Knowing me Knowing God: Exploring your spirituality with Myers-Briggs, 1st Ed, (British Library Cataloguing-in-publication Data, 1994) p.109

the attack. Naturally, the truth is your husband is teaching and preaching the "word" of the living God, the enemy does not like this and he tries to do everything to make life a misery. The Bible declares in (1Peter 5:8), "The devil walks about like a roaring lion, seeking whom he may devour". Therefore we ought to "Be strong in the lord and in the power of His might, putting on the whole armour of God in order to stand against the wiles of the devil" (Ephesians 6:10-11). By "Humbling ourselves before God and drawing close to Him He will draw close to us" (James 4:7-8). Satan is a deceiver. "The moment you became God's child, Satan, like a mobster hit man, puts out a "contract" on you, you are his enemy and he's plotting your down fall".[14] Satan the enemy of God is a liar. Jesus defeated him at Calvary and all authority in heaven and earth belong to Him. This authority is now transferred to believers in the faith. Consequently, let's not put a limit on prayer, because God who is sovereign is not intimidated by the troubles, and situations that may surround us. We must extend our "Faith in Him, whose power will protect us, until the last day. Then He will save us, just as He has always planned to do" (1 Peter 5:3).

For that reason, I urge those of you, who are not praying enough, please make it your priority to

---

14 Rick Warren, The Purpose Driven Life: What on Earth am I Here For? (Zondervan, 2002) p.205

start. It is never too late. Just start from where you are. If you have started please continue to do so. Do not be discouraged in well doing.

"We pray because by intuition or experience, we understand that the most intimate communion with God comes only through prayers".[15]

In (2 Chronicles 7:14) The Lord addresses believers saying,

"If my people who are called by my name will humble themselves, and pray seek His face , turn from their wicked ways then He God will hear from heaven and forgive their sins and heal their land".

This powerful scripture, I believe sums up how we can take hold of God's formula for prayer. The first part of this verse speaks about humbling ourselves. What do we grasp from this? Acknowledging that God is sovereign, He is our king of kings, and Lord of Lords. He is our creator and we must be ready to surrender our all to Him. The next step is seeking the face of God. What do we understand by this? It means that we are going to spend some quality time with the Lord, not a quick fix one or two minute's prayer, even though it has its place, we must be in consistent communication with Him.

---

15 Bill Hybels, Too Busy not to Pray: Slowing Down to be With God, 1st Ed, (Inter-Varsity Press, 2006,) p.11

For example, we need to talk to God about everything we do. Let's take note of David's story. Have you noticed before David goes to battle, He always enquires of the Lord? Saying "Shall I go up to any of the cities of......" (2 Samuel 2:1). Because of this the Lord preserved him wherever he went (2 Samuel 8:14).

Thirdly, we should turn from our wicked ways. What does this mean? We must stop doing the things we know are contrary to the word of God, and start to walk in the way of righteousness. God said if we apply all these principles He will bring healing to our land.

Women of Hope, I implore you to pray without stopping, pray for families, friends, neighbours, the nation at large, do not give up, do not give in until there is break through. As a Christian, when I pray for others, those that I am acquainted with, and those that I am not acquainted with, from personal experience, much blessing is received.

When we pray it helps us to focus on Christ, on the contrary when we don't pray we focus on our state of affairs.

In the book of (Matthew 6:33) Jesus said,

"But seek ye first the kingdom of God and His righteousness and all things shall be added to you".

We must seek to put God first in our lives, and rely on Him to look after our needs. This does not mean that we are going to live a trouble free life, but we will be able to live a life that is peaceful. I believe if we can maintain a life of serenity, we can think clearly, and in doing so, we will be able to accomplish great and wonderful things, which will benefit our community and help one's self and the family.

Results of Prayers

Did you know that God is the one who gives creative ideas? Women of destiny, one idea from the Lord will make a world of difference to humanity. In the year 2001 my husband, the children and I have decided to answer the call of God on our lives. We moved away from a big city, the congregation with which we used to worship was approximately six hundred (600) people. We then moved to a small village approximately 120 miles away, leaving our home, family, our jobs and friends behind to pastor a fellowship of eight (8) members. The church could not afford our expense; therefore, we didn't put the pressure with regard to expense on the fellowship, so we decided to cast our cares upon Jesus because He is our provider.

In (Matthew 6:25-31) Jesus proclaims,

"Therefore I say to you, don't worry about your life, what you eat or drink, or about your body what you put on. Is not life more than meat and the body than raiment? Behold the fowls of the air for they sow not, neither do they reap, nor gather into barns; yet your heavenly Father feedeth them; are ye not much better than they? Which of you by taking thought can add one cubit unto His stature? And why take ye thought for the raiment? Consider the lilies of the field, how they grow; they toil not, neither do they spin; and yet I say unto you, that even Solomon in all his glory was not arrayed like one of these. Wherefore, if God so clothe the grass of the field, which today is, and tomorrow is cast into the oven, shall He not much more clothe you, O ye of little faith? Therefore, I say take no thought saying what you shall eat? Or, what shall we drink? Or wherewithal shall we be clothed?"

How satisfying, and promising are the Words of Jesus, that is revealed in Matthew's Gospel. Did God work miracles? Oh yes He did, in His mercy He gave us creative ideas so that we were able to open our own business, and create employment for others around us. This wasn't an easy task but God who gives innovative ideas turns it into reality, and has made this possible. All we need to do is to obey His command, do what He asks of us and He will do stupendous work in and through us. "God hears and answers prayers for those who obey Him".[16] In scripture we are told, Jacob wrestled with the Angel until his prayer was answered (Genesis.32:25-29). Do you think you can hold on in prayer until you get an answer or until the break of day? Yes it is possible, don't lose hope, don't lose faith and don't lose your vision. "[God] is able to do exceedingly abundantly above all that we ask or think" (Ephesians 3:20).

When we pray it allows God to do the impossible. What did God say to Abraham? In (Genesis 18:14) "Is there anything too hard for God?" This confirms that God is the all-powerful creator, and He is the answer to our world today, if only we would take the time to call on Him in prayer. It doesn't matter what the situation is, how you get there, when you get there and why you are there, God cares so much about us; if only we could make our requests known to Him then He will liberate us and make our path straight. According to (Matthew 7:7), "Ask, and it shall be given to you, seek, and you will find; knock and it will be opened to you".

I truly came to realise all things are possible for God, and there is no problem on this earth that He cannot solve. After all, He is God, it does not

16 Armstrong , G.,T. The Answer to Unanswered prayer, The church of God international Texas USA, 1989, p.113

matter what we think or don't think of Him, He is still God and our ideas of Him will never change who He is.

My prayer is that of Jabez, in Chronicles and that of Paul in Ephesians. I hope for you to pray this prayer too.

"Oh that God will bless me and enlarge my territory that He would keep me from evil, that I may not cause pain" (1 Chronicles 4:10).

"For this reason I bow my knees to the Father of our Lord Jesus Christ. From whom the whole family in heaven and earth is named. That He would grant me, according to the riches of His glory, to be strengthened with might through His Spirit in the inner man, that Christ may dwell in your hearts through faith; that I being rooted and grounded in love, may be able to comprehend with all the saints what is the width and length and depth and height, to know the love of Christ which passes knowledge; that I may be filled with all the fullness of God" (Ephesians 3:14-19).

It was through praying that God spoke to me to pursue the career that I am now doing. I have no regrets, I believe it is the best thing I have ever done. It gives me tremendous joy, and peace of mind, all praise and glory to the Lord Almighty. I have in the past chosen a different profession but God has other plans for my life, and in the end it is for the good.

Jesus speaks out in (Jeremiah 29:11-12),

"For I know the thoughts that I think toward you, says the Lord, thoughts of peace and not of evil, to give you a future and a hope Thus, you will call upon me and pray and I will listen".

Think of all the sorrows, and trials one has been through, sickness and pain. Jesus is saying, the future plans I have for you are awesome. A future that is bright, one in which you can maximise your fullest potentials, a hope of joy and not of sorrows. Just continue to trust Him in the not so easy circumstances. He is able to work all things together for good to those who love Him and to those who are called according to His will and purpose.

According to Acts of the Apostles, It was because of prayer that the prison's doors were opened vigorously for Paul and Silas and both were set free from jail. Even the guard that was guarding the prison's door recognised the power of prayer and fell down at their feet, asking them what he must do to be saved. That night he and his family accepted Jesus as personal saviour.

I also believe prayer along with our faith in God is the key to any problematic situation. In the year 2010, I was talking to a young Christian lady who shared with me the difficulties she was experiencing with her husband. What she told me, was rather disturbing it brought tear drops to my eyes. However, I asked her how she was coping with such a distressing situation. She hastily replied and said she fasted and prayed about it and she felt as though the Lord was carrying her. She said she couldn't look at the problem because she recognised that her husband was not the problem, it was the adversary who used him to do the things that were displeasing to God and the family.

Women of God, it takes a prayerful person to speak like this, somehow God had lifted the heavy load from off her shoulders, by allowing her not to feel the pain. When God carries His children it is such a majestic feeling. A sense of feeling that is outside of this world. It does not matter the shame, and disgrace that surrounds the circumstances, God has taken the pain and give an endless peace. A perpetual peace that is beyond human comprehension, in the course of crisis, when people exclude you, you just cannot respond to the criticism. God, and God alone, had taken all the dilemmas and cares upon Himself. Can anyone fight with God and win? No would be the answer. He remains the Lion of the Tribe of Judah (Revelation 5:5), I am who I am (Exodus 3:14), the everlasting God (Isaiah. 40:28), Wonderful, Counsellor and the Prince of Peace (Isaiah.9:6).

One of the most uplifting poems that encapsulate this feeling is Footprints. It reads;

"One night I dreamed I was walking along the beach with the Lord. Many scenes from my life flashed across the sky. In each scene, I noticed footprints in the sand. Sometimes there were two sets of footprints, other times there was one set of footprints. This bothered me because I noticed that during the low periods of my life, when I was suffering from my anguish, sorrow or defeat, I could see only one set of footprints, so I asked the Lord, You promised me Lord, that if I followed you, you would walk with me always. But I have noticed that during the most trying periods of my life there have only been one set of footprints in the sand. Why, when I needed you most, have you not been there for me? The Lord replied, "The times when you have seen only one set of footprints in the sand, is "when" I carried you".[17]

Woman of destiny, do not magnify your problems, magnify God. Prayer can turn sorrows to triumph. "True prayer is God's chosen means of grace, in prayer God meets us and we build up a living relationship with Him".[18] "The power of prayer moves the hands of God".[19] When we learn to trust God in prayer we are free to reach

---

17 Mary Stephenson (1922-1999)

18 John Woolmer, Thinking clearly about prayer, 1st Ed, (Monarch publication, 1977) p.38

beyond ourselves, to gain insight and understanding of who God is.

In (Ephesians 6:12-13) Paul writes,

"For we do not wrestle against flesh and blood but against principalities against powers against the rulers of the darkness of this age, against spiritual hosts of wickedness in the heavenly places; therefore, take up the whole armour of God that you may be able to withstand in the evil day, and having done all, to stand".

Jesus also declared in (Matthew 18:19). "If two of you agree on earth concerning anything that they ask, it will be done by the father in heaven".

Undoubtedly, we have the power in the name of Jesus to proclaim what we need, according to the power He has invested in us, as long as we obey Him in prayer. How fascinating? In a world of uncertainty and fear, everyone is searching for an answer, the only way we are going to achieve this is right down on our knees in prayer and supplication before God almighty. The battle we face daily is not with people, or situations there is always an enemy who attacks the people of God, but we know in whom we believe, and we are persuaded that He is able to keep us from falling, and He is more than a

---

19 Joyce Meyers, The Power of Simple Prayer: How to Talk To God About Everything, 1st Ed, (Great Britain, 2009,) p.66

conqueror. He is the all powerful God. "He has triumphed gloriously" (Exodus 15:21).

Why are people not praying?

Some of the reasons people suggested for not praying are as follows;

- Afraid of the Unknown

- Time factors

- Unbelief

We should never be afraid to pray, that's where we get our strength. Prayer I believe develops strong character in any person that prays. From experience prayer gives a serenity of mind and certainly a heart of contentment putting troubled souls and minds at peace. "Prayer is designed to work for you, not against you"[20]

I recalled few months ago I was conversing with a friend encouraging her to pray. She liked the idea at first but a few seconds in the conversation she suddenly said to me that when she prays her problems increase. I used to feel this way myself especially in my early walk with the Lord but through continuous fasting, prayer and reading the word of God all fears and doubts are gone.

20 Charles Capps, Releasing The Ability Of God, Great Britain 1978, p.24

Women of hope, the devil would like us to believe negativity, but in order to attain positive results we need to pray without ceasing. We need to get to that place in God and say like Paul in (Romans 8:38-39),

"Who then can separate us from the love of Christ? Can trouble do it, or hardship or persecution or hunger or poverty of danger or death? No, in all these things we have complete victory through Him who loved us. For I am persuaded that neither death or life or angels or principalities or power, or things present or things to come, or height, or depth or any other created, shall be able to separate us from the love of God which is in Christ Jesus our Lord".

Time factors should not be an issue for the people of God. We were born to worship. There is always a "vacuum" inside of us that demands worship, that's how God made us, to worship. Hence, if we don't worship God, we are going to worship something else. Be it an idol therefore, it calls to question we must take time to worship Him in prayer.

This is a question that is often time asked! Why should we pray when God knows and hears us before we asked?

When we pray it shows we are obedient to God's commands, and we know obedience brings blessings. "Abraham was an hundred years old when his son Isaac was born to him" (Genesis 21:5). Jesus himself prayed even more than anyone who ever lived (Matthew 26:39). He prayed in the garden of Gethsemane until His soul was exceedingly sorrowful even to the point of death (Matthew.26:38). He often got up early in the morning (Mark 1:35); late at night (Matthew 14:23) and from time to time all through the night (Luke 6:12) and spent many hours with His father. His disciples were so taken aback with His prayer life they enquired of Him how they should pray.

Jesus taught them in (Matthew 6:9-13),

"Our father which Art in heaven, Hallowed be thy name. Thy kingdom come, Thy will be done, on earth as it is in heaven. Give us this day our daily bread, and forgive us our debts, as we forgive our debtors. And lead us not into temptation, but deliver us from evil: For Thine is the kingdom, and the power, and the glory, forever and ever". Amen.

Having ruminated on the Lord's Prayer, I believe it is of paramount importance that we pray using the words from the Lord's Prayer. It is a model prayer for believers in the faith; it is also intended to meet our every need and covers every area of our well-being. Let us not fail in giving it our fullest meditation.

How else can we communicate with God? It is through prayer. Why are we finding it so hard to pray? Jesus likes to hear us pray, that's what He requires from us, prayer also opens the communication between God and man. If Jesus who is the son of God prays, what should hinder us from praying? Jesus is our prime example. He kept in close contact with His father by praying to Him consistently. In (John 17:15) He says, "I do not pray that you should take them out of the world, but that you should keep them from the evil one".

(Luke 18:1) reminds us,

"Jesus spoke a parable to them that men always ought to pray and not to lose heart".

As believers if we refuse to pray we will then faint, by fainting we will lose focus not knowing what to do. If we do not know what to do, we are losing the vision, by losing our spiritual vision we will suffer defeat. In (Hosea 4:6) Jesus said, "My people are destroyed from lack of knowledge". Lack of know-how means we will be brought to a standstill.

So as faith believers we must find the time to pray, humbling ourselves before God and allowing Him to use us as He wills. "Not my will, but yours, be done" (Luke 22:42). Can you imagine God at sundry times gives us the strength we need, the breath that we breathe.

He is the sustainer of all living beings. Should He decide on taking life from us, we would all die. Why then are we so busy that we can't talk to Him?

Women of God, when I get up and pray early in the morning it gives such strength, such boldness, I feel I can master just about everything that day. When I do not take the time to pray I feel so lethargic, heavy and less work is accomplished that day. There are times when we can pray a quick fix prayer and get result but there are other times when we need to devote ourselves to some serious praying and fasting. Lots of problems may not go away in a quick fix manner; we need to tarry before God in prayer and fasting.

I remembered when I was a young Christian in my teens. We used to have some ladies in church; we called them the "prayer mothers" of Zion. Where are those prayer mothers today? If you were not a Christian, be it biological parents or not, they would take the time out, day by day, week after week, year after year, as often as possible on their knees praying that God will save you from the wrath to come. Did they get results? The answer should be a resounding yes. I am a product of those prayers today, and many more before and after me. God certainly turned situations around by the prayers of a few wholehearted, devoted and faithful women of God who failed to eat and

77

drink until their prayers were answered. "Regardless of the source of any difficulty you have, you have nothing to lose and possibly everything to gain by praying".[21]

"Do not pray for easy lives; pray to be stronger people! Do not pray for tasks equal to your power, pray for power equal to your task. Then the doing of your work shall be no miracle, but you shall be a miracle. Every day you shall wonder at yourself, at the richness of life which has come to you by the grace of God".[22]

In considering seeking how to pray, the main thing we need to be aware of is that prayer is not way out there in the blue somewhere, it is recognizing from our heart that God is sovereign. As we pray the Lord always seems to meet us where we are, and so lovingly cheers us with a word or a song just when we need them most. We should also remember that Jesus is praying for us, He is standing at the throne of grace "interceding" on our behalf (Hebrews 7:25). "Prayer is essential to Christian unity as breath is to the body".[23] Let's keep on praying and believing. Jesus is the only way; He only can satisfy our needs.

---

21 Anderson, N.,T. Steps to freedom in Christ, 1st Ed, United Kingdom, 2003, p.11

22 J. S. Feinbery, Where is God? (Broadman & Holman publisher, 2004) P.108

23 Maxwell Craig, For God's Sake Unity, 1st Ed, (Wild Goose Publications, Glasgow, 1998) P.31

Prayer

You can pray for a moment,
Or for a minute
An hour, a day, or a week,
You can pray when you're strong,
Or when you're sick,
You can pray when you're feeling weak.
You can pray when you're afraid,
Happy or sad,
You can pray when you feel alone.
You can pray with your mother
Father and brother,
By yourself, or over the phone,
But a prayer isn't a time,
A moment, or a person,
A feeling, or a specific place,
A prayer is God's personal way
for giving His, eternal grace.
(Ruth Wright-Palmer 2010)

Encouragement

What is encouragement? Encouragement is an "Inspiration"[24]

The minister's wife is one of those people who seem to give a word of encouragement to those she sets her eyes on. This happens on a regular basis; she sometimes has to forget about her own problems, and lend a helping hand to those in need. Her tears are sometimes near but she often wears a smile to make others happy. Individuals at times look to her for answers; she plays the role of a mother, sister, aunty, friend, and a wife. She often makes herself available for anyone who desires fellowship and support. She is only one person but she tries her very best to make somebody's life cheery. This can be very thorny at times, but the grace of God is always surrounding her. She is cognisant of the fact that "Her help comes from the Lord who made the heavens and the earth" (Psalm 124:8)."[She] is like a tree planted along the riverbank; bearing its fruit in each season without failing; and whatever [she] does shall prosper" (Psalm 1:3). She is certainly a champion among champions, one to look up to, an example for others to follow as well as one to be admired.

---

24 According to Universal Dictionary (1994)

Encouragement

Encouragement can come in the form of a song,

Or the feeling received when things go wrong.

It is like a flight of stairs when you're stuck on the floor,

the light in a tunnel, or an open door,

as a struggler you may feel you cannot go on,

but God sent His only son,

to show us that He'll never let us down;

even when we're still on the ground.

He'll give us the path to carry us through,

He'll give us wings so we can fly

High above our problems so we can succeed

That's His encouragement, that's all we need.

(Ruth Wright-Palmer 2010)

Anointing

"Anointing means to pour oil"[25] (usually olive oil) "Oil is one of the symbols of the Holy Spirit" (Mark 6:13).

The wife of a minister needs to be constantly covered under the blood of Jesus Christ, every second, minute, and every hour on a daily basis by herself, her husband, and other praying believers. She often bears the groan of her husband and others but this is never noticed. Prayer and fasting every so often are her daily food; her pillows at night from time to time are flooded with tears due to the burdens she carries and at morn her face beams with laughter because of the passions she carries for her husband, her children and the ministry. She is a warrior, she is sincere, she is strong-minded, and she is unswerving. "[She] take[s] refuge in the Lord" (Psalm 11:1). He is her rock on which she takes her stand" (Psalm 18:46). And she is capable in accomplishing all things. She lifts her head high and carries a banner marked "victory in Jesus our Saviour forever", on a daily basis. She is none other than a woman of God, full of bliss and who is highly favoured.

---

25 Dennis and Rita Bennett, The Holy Spirit and You, 1st, Ed, (Kingsway Publication. Great Britain, 1985) P.40

Anointing

There is a sweet anointing in this place,

From the one who gave us love and grace.

There is a sweet anointing on our tongues,

To keep singing thankful songs.

There is a sweet anointing on our hands,

To reach and praise the one who ever stands.

There is a sweet anointing on our minds,

So that our thoughts will be pure and kind.

There is a sweet anointing on our spirits,

So our hearts may rejoice, and with worship they are lit.

There is a sweet anointing for those who yearn,

For a saving redeemer and the chance to learn,

All that is possible, to be seen and done,

And to be alongside Him, when the battle is won.

(Ruth Wright-Palmer 2011)

Confidentiality

Confidentiality is "information told in secret or entrusted with the confidence of another".[26]

A minister's wife should remain confidential at all times. While speaking to many women, I observed that they became self conscious and a bit cautious when discussing their everyday needs; and I believe that they were doing this to safeguard their family, as well as their husband's ministry. Who on this earth would like to see their husband fail? I guess not; we would all like our husbands to succeed in everything they do. So as ministers' wives we would try to talk less and pray more, simply, because we don't know who to trust, who to talk to and where to turn to go to for help if needed. This can be very difficult for ministers' wives but this is a very common matter that they have to endure as an everyday experience.

What is the solution? In the light of Proverbs,

"Trust in the Lord with all your heart and lean not on your own understanding; in all your ways acknowledge Him, and He will direct your path" (Proverbs 3:5-6).

"God did not give us the Spirit of timidity but He has given us the spirit of power, love and of a sound mind" (2 Timothy.1:7). Also in

---

26 According to the Universal Dictionary (1994)

(Romans 8:15) Paul admonished us, "For ye have not received the spirit of bondage again to fear; but ye have received the Spirit of adoption, whereby we cry, Abba, Father".

The woman of faith has taken courage in the word of the Lord. She continues to dwell in the secret place of the most high, and abides under the shadow of the almighty (Psalm 91:1). She declares God's love and kindness in the morning and His faithfulness every night (Psalm 92:2). She knows that the Lord, He is God; it is He who has made us and not we ourselves (Psalm 100:3) She will endeavour to trust in the Lord and bring praises and worship to Him daily.

There is nothing more exciting, challenging and pleasing than following Jesus with our whole heart.

Confidentiality

If we prayed for a problem,
That was troubling me,
Would you feel the need to tell others?
Or help my worries be freed.
If I share with you a thought,
About my hopes and dreams,
Would you use it take it as your own?
Or would you help me with my schemes.
If I tell you a secret,
One that nobody knows,
Would you keep it as your own?
Or tell the world what I disclosed
I know of someone who wouldn't
Do all the incorrect things,
He is the Lord of all,
And His ear is what He brings.
He will listen when we are troubled,
And never tell a soul,
He the one we aspire to be like,
From we're young, until we're old.

(Ruth Wright-Palmer 2011)

Endurance

"Endurance is the ability to withstand prolonged hardship".[27]

Endurance is what every minster's wife should aspire after. This is sometimes very problematic to carry out. You are being criticised by others for the way you walk, dress, speak and look etc. Everything and anything can become chatter or gossip. That's why, it is imperative that the Minister's wife be herself. You need not to change for anyone, only line yourself with the word of God. Others need to accept you for who you are, you are unique, incalculable, important and different. In (1 Corinthians 15:10) we are reminded, By the grace of God we are what we are. If you keep changing, you will lose your identity; people will no longer know who you are. You, yourself will become confused about who you are. How sad can that be? Thus, you are who you are in Christ. David put into words you are "Fearfully and wonderfully made" (Psalm 139:14).

Accept constructive criticism and reject destructive ones. There are always people, who will want to ostracise you no matter what, but you are only one person, and you are only living this life once. Do not let anyone or anything bring distraction to you, stay focused and you

---

27 According to the Collins Compact English Dictionary (2002)

will accomplish that which God declares for your life.

In Philippians we are encouraged by scripture, "Not to fret or have any anxiety about anything, but in every circumstance and in everything, by praying and petition with thanksgiving, continue to make your wants known to God" (Philippians 4:6). And according to (Isaiah 40:29-31), "He gives power to those who are tired and worn out, He offers strength to the weak, even youth will become exhausted and young men will give up. But those who wait on the Lord will find new strength, they will fly on wings like eagles, they will run and not grow weary, they will not faint".

Woman of destiny, who eventually becomes a successful woman of God, knows her hope is in the Lord Jesus Christ, and she is confident that Jesus is "Lord of Lords", and "King of Kings" (1Timothy 6:15). Her faith in God will never waiver because she knows that, "Those who trust in the Lord are like Mount Zion which cannot be moved but shall abide forever and the Lord is well able to surround His people from time to time" (Psalm 125:1-2).

Endurance

We may wonder through the wilderness,
Climb a ladder full of sorrow,
We may have a time of pain and stress,
Any our failures may overflow.
We may cry,
We can ache,
Our faith may die,
And we can break.
But from the rain comes the sun,
And from the Lord: everlasting love,
That we must use to endure-
The tough times, and be successful,
And give thanks, forever more.

(Ruth Wright-Palmer 2011)

Summary

The Minister's wife has always been, and still remains, an asset to her husband's ministry. She will always encourage him to ensure that his friendship with members and others remain healthy and pure. So that familiarity does not cause them to lose their respect for him as the man of God. She will also encourage him to avoid spending time alone with members of the opposite sex and to be aware of the language he uses in his day to day communications whether verbally, text messages, email and face book etc. She does not want to see his character tarnished.

Without her his ministry would not be as successful as it is today. "A husband's success is seen in his wife".[28] She remains a warrior, a counsellor, a prayer partner, an encourager to others, she endures hardship once in a while but she never gives up or complains. She is a sister, an aunty, a mother, a grandmother, and a friend, she is only one person but she endeavours to do her best and gives her all. She is committed, sincere, willing and determined to fulfil God's plans for her life, her family and the community at large. She is unique, different, important and valuable, one to recognise and one to, truly, respect. The Bible depicts her as an, "Honourable woman, her husband can trust her, she greatly enhances his life. She will not

---

28 Derek Prince, Husband & Father: Rediscover The Creator's Purpose For Men, (Chosen Book, 2000) p.33

detract from him but help him all his life" (Proverbs 31:10-12). "Long life is in her right hand; in her left hand are riches and honour. Her ways are pleasant ways, and all her paths are peace. She is a tree of life to those who embrace her; those who lay hold of her will be blessed." (Proverbs 3:16-18).

Do not underestimate her, or judge her, or distract her, she is priceless; she is a treasure. She was an ordinary woman who became an extraordinary and an influential woman of destiny and purpose. She is God's gift to her husband anointed by God to watch over him as well as to minister to him in times of need. She remains an excellent wife, who according to (Proverbs 12:4) becomes "the crown of her husband". Pray for her and with her, she is highly favoured, she will continue to trust in the God of her salvation, and surely God indeed will dwell with her. He alone knows her heart and He alone is worthy.

Bibliography

Anderson, N.,T.(2004) Steps to freedom in Christ, 1st Ed, United Kingdom

Armstrong , G.,T. (1989) The Answer to Unanswered prayer, The church of God international Texas USA

Bennett, D., R. (1985) The Holy Spirit and You, 1st, Ed, Kingsway Publication. Great Britain

Capps, C. (1978) Releasing The Ability Of God, Great Britain

Collins English Dictionary (2002) Harper Collins publishers, Great britain

Craig, M. (1998) For God's Sake Unity, 1st Ed, Wild Goose Publications, Glasgow

Feinbery, J., S. (2004) Where is God? Broadman & Holman publisher

Goldsmith, M. (1994) Knowing me Knowing God: Exploring your spirituality with Myers-Briggs, 1st Ed, Great Britain,

Goll, J., W. (2005) The lost Art of Practicing His Presence, Destiny Image Publishers, United state of America

Hoekema, A., A. (1989) Saved by Grace, 1st Ed, the Paternoster Press, united states of America

Hybels, B. (2006) Too busy not to pray: slowing down to be with God, 1st Ed, Inter-Varsity Press.

Meyer, J. (2009) The power of simple prayer: How to talk to God about everything, 1st Ed, Great Britain

Prince, D. (2000) Husbands and Fathers: Rediscover the creator's purpose for men, Chosen Books, Great Britain.

Omartian, S. (1999) Just Enough Light for the step I'm on, 1st Ed, Kingsway Publication Eastbourne

Omartian, S. (2002) The power of a praying woman, Harvest House publisher

The Thompson Chain-Reference Bible, New International Version, (1983) The B.B. Kirkbride Bible Company and the Zondervan Corporation

The Oxford English Dictionary (1973) 3rd Oxford University Press, United Sate

Warren, R. (2002) The purpose driven life: What on earth am I here for? United State of America

White, P. (2000) The Effective Pastor: getting the tools to upgrade your ministry, 1st Ed, Great Britain

Woolmer, J. (1977) Thinking clearly about prayer, 1st Ed, Monarch publication

Universal Dictionary (1994) 1st Ed, London Reader's Digest Association Ltd

Index of Scriptures

Old Testament

Genesis	1:27	2:23
	18:14	21:2-3
	21:5	32:25-29
	39:9	
Exodus	3:14	14:13-14
	15:21	
Numbers	13:18-20	14:31
	23:19	30-31
Joshua	1:9	
Ruth	1:16	
Judges	4:1-2	4:8-9
1 Samuel	16:7	
2 Samuel	2:1	6:11
	8:14	
1 Kings	19:4	
1 Chronicles	4:10	12:32
	14:4	15:10
2 Chronicles	7:14	20:6
	20:15	20:22
Nehemiah	6:3	
Esther	4:15-16	
Psalms	1:3	9:1-2
	11:1	16:11
	18:46	19:14
	20:7-8	21:5-6
	23:1	27:10

Psalms	30:5	34:1
	34:22	37:25
	40:1-2	42:11
	46:11	55:22
	62:6	64:10
	91:1-2	92:3
	100:3	116:1
	117:1-2	124:8
	125:1-2	126:1-2
	128:1-2	139:1-2
	139:14	141:8
Proverbs	3:5-6	3:14-18
	10:22	12:4
	15:1	18:2-22
	25:11	31:10-31
Ecclesiastes	9:11	
Songs of Solomon	2:1	
Isaiah	9:6	40:28
	40:29-31	43:1-3
	43:13	54: 17
Jeremiah	1:5	29:11-12
	33:11	51:20
Hosea	4:6	
Joel	2:26	
Zechariah	1:2-3	4:6

New Testament

Matthew	5:13-14	6:25.31
	6:33	6:9-13
	7:7	11:30
	14:23	16:19
	18:19	19:5-6
	22:42	26:38-39
Mark	1:35	6:13
	7:14-15	
Luke	4:18-19	6:12
	18:1	11:28
	22:42	
John	3: 2-3	4:23-24
	6:48	6:63
	11:14	11:25-26
	14:26	16:13
	17:15	
Acts	1:8	2:1-4
	5:32	10:44
Romans	1:17	8:11
	8:15	8:26-28
	8:31-35	8:38-39
1 Corinthians	14:2	14:4

	15:10	
Galatians	5:22-23	
Ephesians	1:7	1:22
	3:14-20	6:10-13
	6:18	
Philippians	1:6	4:6-7
	4:13	4:19
Colossians	3:3	
Thessalonians	5:21-22	
1 Timothy	6:15	
2 Timothy	1:7	
Hebrews	7:25	13:5
James	1:2-3	4:7-8
	4:17	5:16-18
1 Peter	2:9	3:3-4
	3:6	5:3
	5:7-8	
1 John	3:2-3	5:15
Revelation	5:5	21:6
	22:16	

www.ingramcontent.com/pod-product-compliance
Lightning Source LLC
Chambersburg PA
CBHW051841040426

42447CB00006B/642